Walter Brueggemann's BIG Imagination

A BIOGRAPHY FOR CHILDREN

Written by
Conrad L. Kanagy

Illustrated by
Audrey Kanagy

Walter Brueggemann's Big Imagination
A Biography for Children
by Conrad Kanagy

Copyright © 2023
All rights reserved.

All rights reserved. Reproduction or utilization of this work in any form, by any means now known or herein after invented, including but not limited to xerography, photocopying and recording, and in any storage and retrieval system, is forbidden without permission from the copyrighted holder.

International Standard Book Number: 978-1-60126-896-9

Masthof Press
219 Mill Road | Morgantown, PA 19543-9516
www.Masthof.com

Walter always felt little. His brother Ed was bigger, older, and stronger. Ed talked a lot and made people laugh. Walter was shy and stood behind his mother.

Ed sometimes disobeyed his parents.
Walter tried very hard to be good.

Walter's favorite pet was Flossie, the cat. Ed's was their big dog named "Nero." While Ed teased Nero until he barked and growled, Walter quietly held Flossie on his lap as she purred with contentment.

When Walter was old enough, he tried to play kickball and other games with the neighborhood boys. But they usually picked him last for their team or told him to go home!

Everything Walter tried to do reminded him that he was little. He felt little on the outside and on the inside.

He couldn't wait to be big.
Like Ed.
Like the other boys.

Walter's father, August, was a pastor who spent time with people whom others ignored. He didn't care if they went to church or not. He brought them home to eat. He found places for them to sleep. He listened to their sad stories. Walter saw how important his father was to these people. He always felt a "wee bit" bigger when he was with his dad.

Sometimes people from the town and church said unkind things about Walter's dad. They thought he spent too much time with the wrong people. "Shouldn't he care most about church people?"

Walter's dad didn't care if others disliked him. He had learned to treat people as he wanted to be treated. He told Walter that everyone had reasons why they were grumpy, mean, unkind, or sad.

Walter discovered that he loved to read. He read "like a beaver!" But his school only had a few books. He read them over and over again. One day, the school librarian brought an armful of new books from the town library. It was one of the best days of Walter's life!

Walter learned that he was good with words—writing words, reading words, putting words together, and speaking words. He felt a "wee bit" bigger when he was with stories and words.

Words and stories took him places he had never been before. He forgot what others said about his father. He forgot what others said about him. He forgot how little he was.

In Walter's church, children had to study for two years before joining the congregation. They memorized hundreds of Bible verses from a little book called the Catechism. They took a test at the end. Walter did better than anyone else!

Walter's father gave each child a Bible verse to remember that special day. He gave Walter: "God's words are a lamp to guide me and a light for the road ahead of me" (Psalm 119:105). When Walter was an old man he would say, "My dad sure got it right. I have been with God's words every day of my life!"

Like his father, Walter spent his life helping others. He taught his students to love God's words like he did. He taught them to care about the poor, the forgotten, and the disliked just like his father had. He preached that God was big and did big things.

Walter told his students that some people didn't believe God's words were true. He said they had small imaginations. "Remember when you were little and everything else seemed so big?" he asked. "Sometimes when we grow big, our imaginations grow small. Then we forget how big God is."

When Walter preached God's words, he felt bigger. When he wrote books about God's words, he felt bigger. When he studied God's words he felt bigger. He also seemed bigger to those around him when he was doing those things.

By the time Walter was an old man, he had written more than one hundred books. All his books had one thing in common. They told the stories of people from the Bible who had big imaginations about their big God!

There were still days when Walter felt little. He wondered if he had written enough books. If he could have written better books. If he had done enough big things with his life. If he had been good enough.

But he began to understand that feeling little had nothing to do with how old or tall he was. Or how much he had done. Or how good he was. He remembered the Bible stories he loved, where God used little people and those who felt little inside. Why? Because they needed a big God. It was the little people who still had big imaginations.

Walter realized that a big imagination is what the Bible describes as faith. And though he was old and often tired, Walter knew that his big imagination remained, even when he was feeling his littlest! And so did his faith in a big God who loved him just as he was!

THE END

Conrad L. Kanagy, PhD is Prof. of sociology at Elizabethtown College and a retired Mennonite pastor. He is the author of the biography of theologian Walter Brueggemann entitled *The Prophetic Imagination of Walter Brueggemann: A Theological Biography*, (Fortress Press, 2023) and the editor of three forthcoming books by Brueggemann. Conrad and his wife, Heidi, are the grandparents of Ezra and Levi.

Audrey A. Kanagy has enjoyed and employed her artist talent throughout her life in many different roles including camping ministry, pastoral ministry, teaching, and currently, helping senior citizens enjoy life to the fullest.

Walter Brueggemann is William Marcellus McPheeters Professor of Old Testament Emeritus at Columbia Theological Seminary. He is the world's leading interpreter of the Old Testament.

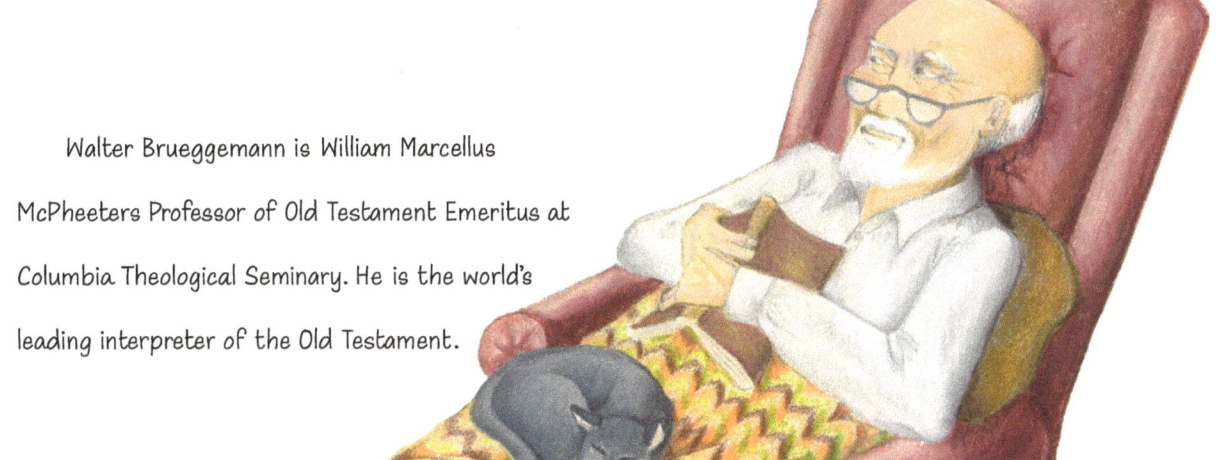

www.ingramcontent.com/pod-product-compliance
Lightning Source LLC
Chambersburg PA
CBHW040007080526
44586CB00027B/2910